STRING QUARTETS
BY DEBUSSY AND RAVEL

Claude Debussy
Quartet in G Minor, Op. 10

Maurice Ravel
Quartet in F Major

DOVER PUBLICATIONS, INC.

NEW YORK

String Quartets by Debussy and Ravel is a new selection of works, first published by Dover Publications, Inc., in 1987. The Debussy quartet is an unabridged republication of the work first published by Durand, Paris, 1894. The Ravel quartet is an unabridged republication of the work first published by Astruc, Paris, 1904 [1903?] (revised edition, Durand, Paris, 1910). The Glossary of French Terms has been specially prepared for the present edition.

The publisher is grateful to the George Sherman Dickinson Music Library of Vassar College for making its material available for reproduction.

Manufactured in the United States of America
Dover Publications, Inc., 31 East 2nd Street, Mineola, N.Y. 11501

Library of Congress Cataloging-in-Publication Data

Debussy, Claude, 1862–1918.
  [Quartet, strings, op. 10, G minor]
  String quartets.

  Reprint (1st work). Originally published: Paris : Durand, 1894.
  Reprint (2nd work). Originally published: Paris : Astruc, 1903 or 1904.
  Contents: First quartet in G minor, op. 10 / Claude Debussy—Quartet in F major / Maurice Ravel.
  1. String quartets—Scores.   I. Ravel, Maurice, 1875–1937. Quartet, strings, F major. 1986.
M452.D281 op. 10 1986   86-751911
ISBN 0-486-25231-0

Contents

Glossary of French Terms

agité: agitato
alto: viola
animé: lively
assez vif et bien rythmé: quite spiritedly and rhythmically
augmentez: crescendo
aussi . . . que possible: as . . . as possible
avec passion: with passion
bien chanté: molto cantabile
calme: calm
cédez: slacken
décidé: firmly
doux, doucement: soft, softly
du talon: with the nut of the bow
en animant: becoming livelier
en dehors: prominently
en diminuant: diminuendo
énergique: energetic
en s'affaiblissant: diminuendo
en s'éloignant: growing distant
en serrant: speeding up, stringendo
et: and
expressif: expressive
jusqu'à la fin: up to the end
léger, lég(èremen)t: lightly
marqué: marcato
même: same
mettez: put (on)

modéré: moderate
modérément: moderately
mouv(emen)t: tempo
mouvementé: lively
ôtez: remove
passioné: impassioned
pas trop: not too
peu: little
peu à peu: gradually
plus: more
pressez: speed up, stringendo
retenu: ritenuto
sans ralentir: without slackening (the pace)
serrez: speed up, stringendo
sourdine: mute
soutenu: sostenuto
suivez: colla parte
sur la touche: on the fingerboard, sulla tastiera
toujours: always
tranquille: tranquil
très: very
un peu: a little
vif: spirited
violon: violin
violoncelle: cello
vite: quickly

Claude Debussy
QUARTET IN G MINOR, Op. 10

I

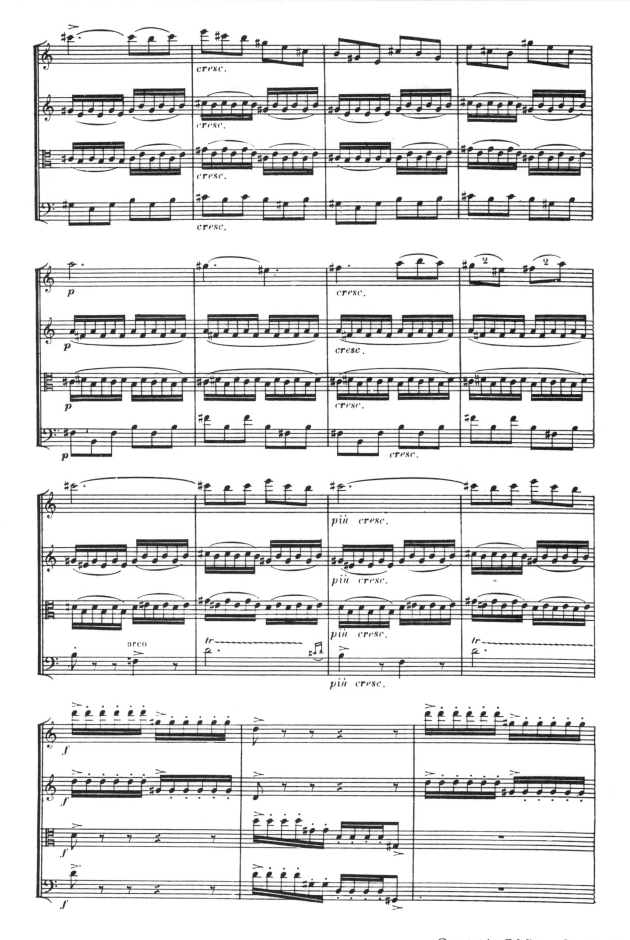

III

IV

Maurice Ravel
QUARTET IN F MAJOR

I

II

Assez vif – Très rythmé (♩. = 92)

III

Très lent (♩ = 44)

IV

FIN

Dover Chamber Music Scores

COMPLETE SUITES FOR UNACCOMPANIED CELLO AND SONATAS FOR VIOLA DA GAMBA, Johann Sebastian Bach. Bach-Gesellschaft edition of the six cello suites (BWV 1007–1012) and three sonatas (BWV 1027–1029), commonly played today on the cello. 112pp. 9⅜ × 12¼. 25641-3 Pa. **$7.95**

WORKS FOR VIOLIN, Johann Sebastian Bach. Complete Sonatas and Partitas for Unaccompanied Violin; Six Sonatas for Violin and Clavier. Bach-Gesellschaft edition. 158pp. 9⅜ × 12¼. 23683-8 Pa. **$7.95**

COMPLETE STRING QUARTETS, Wolfgang A. Mozart. Breitkopf & Härtel edition. All 23 string quartets plus alternate slow movement to K.156. Study score. 277pp. 9⅜ × 12¼. 22372-8 Pa. **$11.95**

COMPLETE STRING QUINTETS, Wolfgang Amadeus Mozart. All the standard-instrumentation string quintets, plus String Quintet in C Minor, K.406; Quintet with Horn or Second Cello, K.407; and Clarinet Quintet, K.581. Breitkopf & Härtel edition. Study score. 181pp. 9⅜ × 12¼. 23603-X Pa. **$8.95**

STRING QUARTETS, OPP. 20 and 33, COMPLETE, Joseph Haydn. Complete reproductions of the 12 masterful quartets (six each) of Opp. 20 and 33—in the reliable Eulenburg edition. 272pp. 8⅜ × 11¼. 24852-6 Pa. **$11.95**

STRING QUARTETS, OPP. 42, 50 and 54, Joseph Haydn. Complete reproductions of Op. 42 in D minor; Op. 50, Nos. 1–6 ("Prussian Quartets") and Op. 54, Nos. 1–3. Reliable Eulenburg edition. 224pp. 8⅜ × 11¼. 24262-5 Pa. **$9.95**

TWELVE STRING QUARTETS, Joseph Haydn. 12 often-performed works: Op. 55, Nos. 1–3 (including *Razor*); Op. 64, Nos. 1–6; Op. 71, Nos. 1–3. Definitive Eulenburg edition. 288pp. 8⅜ × 11¼. 23933-0 Pa. **$10.95**

ELEVEN LATE STRING QUARTETS, Joseph Haydn. Complete reproductions of Op. 74, Nos. 1–3; Op. 76, Nos. 1–6; and Op. 77, Nos. 1 and 2. Definitive Eulenburg edition. Full-size study score. 320pp. 8⅜ × 11¼. 23753-2 Pa. **$10.95**

COMPLETE STRING QUARTETS, Ludwig van Beethoven. Breitkopf & Härtel edition. Six quartets of Opus 18; three quartets of Opus 59; Opera 74, 95, 127, 130, 131, 132, 135 and Grosse Fuge. Study score. 434pp. 9⅜ × 12¼. 22361-2 Pa. **$15.95**

SIX GREAT PIANO TRIOS IN FULL SCORE, Ludwig van Beethoven. Definitive Breitkopf & Härtel edition of Beethoven's Piano Trios Nos. 1–6 including the "Ghost" and the "Archduke". 224pp. 9⅜ × 12¼. 25398-8 Pa. **$10.95**

COMPLETE VIOLIN SONATAS, Ludwig van Beethoven. All ten sonatas including the "Kreutzer" and "Spring" sonatas in the definitive Breitkopf & Härtel edition. 256pp. 9 × 12. 26277-4 Pa. **$12.95**

COMPLETE SONATAS AND VARIATIONS FOR CELLO AND PIANO, Ludwig van Beethoven. All five sonatas and three sets of variations. Reprinted from Breitkopf & Härtel edition. 176pp. 9⅜ × 12¼. 26441-6 Pa. **$9.95**

COMPLETE CHAMBER MUSIC FOR STRINGS, Franz Schubert. Reproduced from famous Breitkopf & Härtel edition: Quintet in C Major (1828), 15 quartets and two trios for violin(s), viola, and violincello. Study score. 348pp. 9 × 12. 21463-X Pa. **$13.95**

COMPLETE CHAMBER MUSIC FOR PIANOFORTE AND STRINGS, Franz Schubert. Breitkopf & Härtel edition. *Trout*, Quartet in F Major, and trios for piano, violin, cello. Study score. 192pp. 9 × 12. 21527-X Pa. **$9.95**

CHAMBER WORKS FOR PIANO AND STRINGS, Felix Mendelssohn. Eleven of the composer's best known works in the genre—duos, trios, quartets and a sextet—reprinted from authoritative Breitkopf & Härtel edition. 384pp. 9⅜ × 12¼. 26117-4 Pa. **$15.95**

COMPLETE CHAMBER MUSIC FOR STRINGS, Felix Mendelssohn. All of Mendelssohn's chamber music: Octet, Two Quintets, Six Quartets, and Four Pieces for String Quartet. (Nothing with piano is included). Complete works edition (1874–7). Study score. 283pp. 9⅜ × 12¼. 23679-X Pa. **$12.95**

CHAMBER MUSIC OF ROBERT SCHUMANN, edited by Clara Schumann. Superb collection of three trios, four quartets, and piano quintet. Breitkopf & Härtel edition. 288pp. 9⅜ × 12¼. 24101-7 Pa. **$12.95**

COMPLETE SONATAS FOR SOLO INSTRUMENT AND PIANO, Johannes Brahms. All seven sonatas—three for violin, two for cello and two for clarinet (or viola)—reprinted from the authoritative Breitkopf & Härtel edition. 208pp. 9 × 12. 26091-7 Pa. **$10.95**

COMPLETE CHAMBER MUSIC FOR STRINGS AND CLARINET QUINTET, Johannes Brahms. Vienna Gesellschaft der Musikfreunde edition of all quartets, quintets, and sextet without piano. Study edition. 262pp. 8⅜ × 11¼. 21914-3 Pa. **$10.95**

QUINTET AND QUARTETS FOR PIANO AND STRINGS, Johannes Brahms. Full scores of *Quintet in F Minor*, Op. 34; *Quartet in G Minor*, Op. 25; *Quartet in A Major*, Op. 26; *Quartet in C Minor*, Op. 60. Breitkopf & Härtel edition. 298pp. 9 × 12. 24900-X Pa. **$12.95**

COMPLETE PIANO TRIOS, Johannes Brahms. All five piano trios in the definitive Breitkopf & Härtel edition. 288pp. 9 × 12. 25769-X Pa. **$12.95**

CHAMBER WORKS FOR PIANO AND STRINGS, Antonín Dvořák. Society editions of the F Minor and Dumky piano trios, D Major and E-flat Major piano quartets and A Major piano quintet. 352pp. 8⅜ × 11¼. (Available in U.S. only) 25663-4 Pa. **$13.95**

FIVE LATE STRING QUARTETS, Antonín Dvořák. Treasury of Czech master's finest chamber works: Nos. 10, 11, 12, 13, 14. Reliable Simrock editions. 282pp. 8⅜ × 11. 25135-7 Pa. **$11.95**

STRING QUARTETS BY DEBUSSY AND RAVEL/Claude Debussy: Quartet in G Minor, Op. 10/Maurice Ravel: Quartet in F Major, Claude Debussy and Maurice Ravel. Authoritative one-volume edition of two influential masterpieces noted for individuality, delicate and subtle beauties. 112pp. 8⅜ × 11. 25231-0 Pa. **$6.95**

GREAT CHAMBER WORKS, César Franck. Four Great works: Violin Sonata in A Major, Piano Trio in F-sharp Minor, String Quartet in D Major and Piano Quintet in F Minor. From J. Hamelle, Paris and C. F. Peters, Leipzig editions. 248pp. 9⅜ × 12¼. 26546-3 Pa. **$13.95**

*Available from your music dealer or write for **free** Music Catalog to*
Dover Publications, Inc., Dept. MUBI, 31 East 2nd Street, Mineola, N.Y. 11501.

Dover Piano and Keyboard Editions

THE WELL-TEMPERED CLAVIER: Books I and II, Complete, Johann Sebastian Bach. All 48 preludes and fugues in all major and minor keys. Authoritative Bach-Gesellschaft edition. Explanation of ornaments in English, tempo indications, music corrections. 208pp. 9⅜ × 12¼. 24532-2 Pa. **$8.95**

KEYBOARD MUSIC, J. S. Bach. Bach-Gesellschaft edition. For harpsichord, piano, other keyboard instruments. English Suites, French Suites, Six Partitas, Goldberg Variations, Two-Part Inventions, Three-Part Sinfonias. 312pp. 8⅛ × 11. 22360-4 Pa. **$10.95**

ITALIAN CONCERTO, CHROMATIC FANTASIA AND FUGUE AND OTHER WORKS FOR KEYBOARD, Johann Sebastian Bach. Sixteen of Bach's best-known, most-performed and most-recorded works for the keyboard, reproduced from the authoritative Bach-Gesellschaft edition. 112pp. 9 × 12. 25387-2 Pa. **$7.95**

COMPLETE KEYBOARD TRANSCRIPTIONS OF CONCERTOS BY BAROQUE COMPOSERS, Johann Sebastian Bach. Sixteen concertos by Vivaldi, Telemann and others, transcribed for solo keyboard instruments. Bach-Gesellschaft edition. 128pp. 9⅜ × 12¼. 25529-8 Pa. **$7.95**

ORGAN MUSIC, J. S. Bach. Bach-Gesellschaft edition. 93 works. 6 Trio Sonatas, German Organ Mass, Orgelbüchlein, Six Schubler Chorales, 18 Choral Preludes. 357pp. 8⅛ × 11. 22359-0 Pa. **$12.50**

COMPLETE PRELUDES AND FUGUES FOR ORGAN, Johann Sebastian Bach. All 25 of Bach's complete sets of preludes and fugues (i.e. compositions written as pairs), from the authoritative Bach-Gesellschaft edition. 168pp. 8⅜ × 11. 24816-X Pa. **$8.95**

TOCCATAS, FANTASIAS, PASSACAGLIA AND OTHER WORKS FOR ORGAN, J. S. Bach. Over 20 best-loved works including Toccata and Fugue in D minor, BWV 565; Passacaglia and Fugue in C minor, BWV 582, many more. Bach-Gesellschaft edition. 176pp. 9 × 12. 25403-8 Pa. **$9.95**

TWO- AND THREE-PART INVENTIONS, J. S. Bach. Reproduction of original autograph ms. Edited by Eric Simon. 62pp. 8⅛ × 11. 21982-8 Pa. **$5.95**

THE 36 FANTASIAS FOR KEYBOARD, Georg Philipp Telemann. Graceful compositions by 18th-century master. 1923 Breslauer edition. 80pp. 8⅛ × 11. 25365-1 Pa. **$4.95**

GREAT KEYBOARD SONATAS, Carl Philipp Emanuel Bach. Comprehensive two-volume edition contains 51 sonatas by second, most important son of Johann Sebastian Bach. Originality, rich harmony, delicate workmanship. Authoritative French edition. Total of 384pp. 8⅜ × 11¼. Series I 24853-4 Pa. **$8.95**
Series II 24854-2 Pa. **$8.95**

KEYBOARD WORKS/Series One: Ordres I–XIII; Series Two: Ordres XIV–XXVII and Miscellaneous Pieces, François Couperin. Over 200 pieces. Reproduced directly from edition prepared by Johannes Brahms and Friedrich Chrysander. Total of 496pp. 8⅛ × 11.
Series I 25795-9 Pa. **$9.95**
Series II 25796-7 Pa. **$9.95**

KEYBOARD WORKS FOR SOLO INSTRUMENTS, G. F. Handel. 35 neglected works from Handel's vast oeuvre, originally jotted down as improvisations. Includes Eight Great Suites, others. New sequence. 174pp. 9⅜ × 12¼. 24338-9 Pa. **$8.95**

WORKS FOR ORGAN AND KEYBOARD, Jan Pieterszoon Sweelinck. Nearly all of early Dutch composer's difficult-to-find keyboard works. Chorale variations; toccatas, fantasias; variations on secular, dance tunes. Also, incomplete and/or modified works, plus fantasia by John Bull. 272pp. 9 × 12. 24935-2 Pa. **$11.95**

ORGAN WORKS, Dietrich Buxtehude. Complete organ works of extremely influential pre-Bach composer. Toccatas, preludes, chorales, more. Definitive Breitkopf & Härtel edition. 320pp. 8⅜ × 11¼. (Available in U.S. only) 25682-0 Pa. **$11.95**

THE FUGUES ON THE MAGNIFICAT FOR ORGAN OR KEYBOARD, Johann Pachelbel. 94 pieces representative of Pachelbel's magnificent contribution to keyboard composition; can be played on the organ, harpsichord or piano. 100pp. 9 × 12. (Available in U.S. only) 25037-7 Pa. **$6.95**

MY LADY NEVELLS BOOKE OF VIRGINAL MUSIC, William Byrd. 42 compositions in modern notation from 1591 ms. For any keyboard instrument. 245pp. 8⅛ × 11. 22246-2 Pa. **$12.50**

ELIZABETH ROGERS HIR VIRGINALL BOOKE, edited with calligraphy by Charles J. F. Cofone. All 112 pieces from noted 1656 manuscript, most never before published. Composers include Thomas Brewer, William Byrd, Orlando Gibbons, etc. 125pp. 9 × 12.
23138-0 Pa. **$8.95**

THE FITZWILLIAM VIRGINAL BOOK, edited by J. Fuller Maitland, W. B. Squire. Famous early 17th-century collection of keyboard music, 300 works by Morley, Byrd, Bull, Gibbons, etc. Modern notation. Total of 938pp. 8⅜ × 11. Two-vol. set.
21068-5, 21069-3 Pa. **$31.90**

GREAT KEYBOARD SONATAS, Series I and Series II, Domenico Scarlatti. 78 of the most popular sonatas reproduced from the G. Ricordi edition edited by Alessandro Longo. Total of 320pp. 8⅛ × 11¼.
Series I 24996-4 Pa. **$7.95**
Series II 25003-2 Pa. **$7.95**

SONATAS AND FANTASIES FOR THE PIANO, W. A. Mozart, edited by Nathan Broder. Finest, most accurate edition, based on autographs and earliest editions. 19 sonatas, plus Fantasy and Fugue in C, K.394, Fantasy in C Minor, K.396, Fantasy in D Minor, K.397. 352pp. 9 × 12. (Available in U.S. only) 25417-8 Pa. **$14.95**

COMPLETE PIANO SONATAS, Joseph Haydn. 52 sonatas reprinted from authoritative Breitkopf & Härtel edition. Extremely clear and readable; ample space for notes, analysis. 464pp. 9⅜ × 12¼.
24726-0 Pa. **$9.95**
24727-9 Pa. **$10.95**

BAGATELLES, RONDOS AND OTHER SHORTER WORKS FOR PIANO, Ludwig van Beethoven. Most popular and most performed shorter works, including Rondo a capriccio in G and Andante in F. Breitkopf & Härtel edition. 128pp. 9⅜ × 12¼. 25392-9 Pa. **$8.95**

COMPLETE VARIATIONS FOR SOLO PIANO, Ludwig van Beethoven. Contains all 21 sets of Beethoven's piano variations, including the extremely popular *Diabelli Variations, Op. 120.* 240pp. 9⅜ × 12¼. 25188-8 Pa. **$11.95**

COMPLETE PIANO SONATAS, Ludwig van Beethoven. All sonatas in fine Schenker edition, with fingering, analytical material. One of best modern editions. 615pp. 9 × 12. Two-vol. set. (Available in U.S. only) 23134-8, 23135-6 Pa. **$23.90**

COMPLETE SONATAS FOR PIANOFORTE SOLO, Franz Schubert. All 15 sonatas. Breitkopf and Härtel edition. 293pp. 9⅜ × 12¼.
22647-6 Pa. **$12.95**

DANCES FOR SOLO PIANO, Franz Schubert. Over 350 waltzes, minuets, landler, ecossaises, other charming, melodic dance compositions reprinted from the authoritative Breitkopf & Härtel edition. 192pp. 9⅜ × 12¼. 26107-7 Pa. **$8.95**

*Available from your music dealer or write for **free** Music Catalog to*
Dover Publications, Inc., Dept. MUBI, 31 East 2nd Street, Mineola, N.Y. 11501.

Dover Piano and Keyboard Editions

ORGAN WORKS, César Franck. Composer's best-known works for organ, including Six Pieces, Trois Pieces, and Trois Chorals. Oblong format for easy use at keyboard. Authoritative Durand edition. 208pp. 11⅜ × 8¼. 25517-4 Pa. **$9.95**

IBERIA AND ESPAÑA: Two Complete Works for Solo Piano, Isaac Albeniz. Spanish composer's greatest piano works in authoritative editions. Includes the popular "Tango". 192pp. 9 × 12. 25367-8 Pa. **$9.95**

GOYESCAS, SPANISH DANCES AND OTHER WORKS FOR SOLO PIANO, Enrique Granados. Great Spanish composer's most admired, most performed suites for the piano, in definitive Spanish editions. 176pp. 9 × 12. 25481-X Pa. **$8.95**

SELECTED PIANO COMPOSITIONS, César Franck, edited by Vincent d'Indy. Outstanding selection of influential French composer's piano works, including early pieces and the two masterpieces—Prelude, Choral and Fugue; and Prelude, Aria and Finale. Ten works in all. 138pp. 9 × 12. 23269-7 Pa. **$9.95**

THE COMPLETE PRELUDES AND ETUDES FOR PIANOFORTE SOLO, Alexander Scriabin. All the preludes and études including many perfectly spun miniatures. Edited by K. N. Igumnov and Y. I. Mil'shteyn. 250pp. 9 × 12. 22919-X Pa. **$10.95**

COMPLETE PIANO SONATAS, Alexander Scriabin. All ten of Scriabin's sonatas, reprinted from an authoritative early Russian edition. 256pp. 8⅜ × 11¼. 25850-5 Pa. **$9.95**

COMPLETE PRELUDES AND ETUDES-TABLEAUX, Serge Rachmaninoff. Forty-one of his greatest works for solo piano, including the riveting C minor, G-minor and B-minor preludes, in authoritative editions. 208pp. 8⅜ × 11¼. (Available in U.S. only) 25696-0 Pa. **$9.95**

COMPLETE PIANO SONATAS, Sergei Prokofiev. Definitive Russian edition of nine sonatas (1907–1953), among the most important compositions in the modern piano repertoire. 288pp. 8⅜ × 11¼. (Available in U.S. only) 25689-8 Pa. **$10.95**

GYMNOPEDIES, GNOSSIENNES AND OTHER WORKS FOR PIANO, Erik Satie. The largest Satie collection of piano works yet published, 17 in all, reprinted from the original French editions. 176pp. 9 × 12. 25978-1 Pa. **$8.95**

TWENTY SHORT PIECES FOR PIANO (Sports et Divertissements), Erik Satie. French master's brilliant thumbnail sketches—verbal and musical—of various outdoor sports and amusements. English translations, 20 illustrations. Rare, limited 1925 edition. 48pp. 12 × 8⅜. 24365-6 Pa. **$4.95**

COMPLETE PRELUDES, IMPROMPTUS AND VALSES-CAPRICES, Gabriel Fauré. Eighteen elegantly wrought piano works in authoritative editions. Only one-volume collection. 144pp. 9 × 12. 25789-4 Pa. **$7.95**

PIANO MUSIC OF BÉLA BARTÓK, Series I, Béla Bartók. New, definitive Archive Edition incorporating composer's corrections. Includes Funeral March from Kossuth, Fourteen Bagatelles, Bartók's break to modernism. 167pp. 9 × 12. (Available in U.S. only) 24108-4 Pa. **$9.95**

PIANO MUSIC OF BÉLA BARTÓK, Series II, Béla Bartók. Second in the Archie Edition incorporating composer's corrections. 85 short pieces For Children, Two Elegies, Two Rumanian Dances, etc. 192pp. 9 × 12. (Available in U.S. only) 24109-2 Pa. **$9.95**

FRENCH PIANO MUSIC, AN ANTHOLOGY, edited by Isidor Phillipp. 44 complete works, 1670–1905, by Lully, Couperin, Rameau, Alkan, Saint-Saëns, Delibes, Bizet, Godard, many others; favorites, lesser-known examples, but all top quality. 188pp. 9 × 12. 23381-2 Pa. **$8.95**

NINETEENTH-CENTURY EUROPEAN PIANO MUSIC: UNFAMILIAR MASTERWORKS, edited by John Gillespie. Difficult-to-find études, toccatas, polkas, impromptus, waltzes, etc., by Albéniz, Bizet, Chabrier, Fauré, Smetana, Richard Strauss, Wagner and 16 other composers. 62 pieces. 343pp. 9 × 12. 23447-9 Pa. **$15.95**

RARE MASTERPIECES OF RUSSIAN PIANO MUSIC: Eleven Pieces by Glinka, Balakirev, Glazunov and Others, edited by Dmitry Feofanov. Glinka's Prayer, Balakirev's Reverie, Liapunov's Transcendental Etude, Op. 11, No. 10, and eight others—full, authoritative scores from Russian texts. 144pp. 9 × 12. 24659-0 Pa. **$7.95**

NINETEENTH-CENTURY AMERICAN PIANO MUSIC, edited by John Gillespie. 40 pieces by 27 American composers: Gottschalk, Victor Herbert, Edward MacDowell, William Mason, Ethelbert Nevin, others. 323pp. 9 × 12. 23602-1 Pa. **$14.95**

PIANO MUSIC, Louis M. Gottschalk. 26 pieces (including covers) by early 19th-century American genius. "Bamboula," "The Banjo," other Creole, Negro-based material, through elegant salon music. 301pp. 9¼ × 12. 21683-7 Pa. **$12.95**

SOUSA'S GREAT MARCHES IN PIANO TRANSCRIPTION, John Philip Sousa. Playing edition includes: "The Stars and Stripes Forever," "King Cotton," "Washington Post," much more. 24 illustrations. 111pp. 9 × 12. 23132-1 Pa. **$6.95**

COMPLETE PIANO RAGS, Scott Joplin. All 38 piano rags by the acknowledged master of the form, reprinted from the publisher's original editions complete with sheet music covers. Introduction by David A. Jasen. 208pp. 9 × 12. 25807-6 Pa. **$8.95**

RAGTIME REDISCOVERIES, selected by Trebor Jay Tichenor. 64 unusual rags demonstrate diversity of style, local tradition. Original sheet music. 320pp. 9 × 12. 23776-1 Pa. **$11.95**

RAGTIME RARITIES, edited by Trebor J. Tichenor. 63 tuneful, rediscovered piano rags by 51 composers (or teams). Does not duplicate selections in Classic Piano Rags (Dover, 20469-3). 305pp. 9 × 12. 23157-7 Pa. **$12.95**

CLASSIC PIANO RAGS, selected with an introduction by Rudi Blesh. Best ragtime music (1897–1922) by Scott Joplin, James Scott, Joseph F. Lamb, Tom Turpin, nine others. 364pp. 9 × 12. 20469-3 Pa. **$14.95**

RAGTIME GEMS: Original Sheet Music for 25 Ragtime Classics, edited by David A. Jasen. Includes original sheet music and covers for 25 rags, including three of Scott Joplin's finest: Searchlight Rag, Rose Leaf Rag and Fig Leaf Rag. 122pp. 9 × 12. 25248-5 Pa. **$7.95**

MY FIRST BOOK OF MARCHES, Dolly M. Moon. 25 marches in easy piano arrangements: "Stars and Stripes Forever," "Dixie," Schubert's "Marche Militaire," much more. 48pp. 8¼ × 11. 26338-X Pa. **$3.50**

ZEZ CONFREY PIANO SOLOS, RAGTIME, NOVELTY & JAZZ, Belwin Mills. 90 great hits of famed piano composer: "Kitten on the Keys," "Dizzy Fingers," "Giddy Ditty," many others. 329pp. 9 × 12. 24681-7 Pa. **$22.50**

MY VERY FIRST BOOK OF COWBOY SONGS, Dolly Moon. 21 favorites arranged for little hands. "Red River Valley," "My Darling Clementine," 19 more. Illustrated with Remington prints. 46pp. 8¼ × 11. 24311-7 Pa. **$3.50**

SELECTED PIANO WORKS FOR FOUR HANDS, Franz Schubert. 24 separate pieces (16 most popular titles): Three Military Marches, Lebensstürme, Four Polonaises, Four Ländler, etc. Rehearsal numbers added. 273pp. 9 × 12. 23529-7 Pa. **$10.95**

Dover Piano and Keyboard Editions

SHORTER WORKS FOR PIANOFORTE SOLO, Franz Schubert. All piano music except Sonatas, Dances, and a few unfinished pieces. Contains Wanderer, Impromptus, Moments Musicals, Variations, Scherzi, etc. Breitkopf and Härtel edition. 199pp. 9⅜ × 12¼. 22648-4 Pa. **$9.95**

WALTZES AND SCHERZOS, Frédéric Chopin. All of the Scherzos and nearly all (20) of the Waltzes from the authoritative Paderewski edition. Editorial commentary. 214pp. 9 × 12. (Available in U.S. only) 24316-8 Pa. **$9.95**

COMPLETE PRELUDES AND ETUDES FOR SOLO PIANO, Frédéric Chopin. All 26 Preludes, all 27 Etudes by greatest composer of piano music. Authoritative Paderewski edition. 224pp. 9 × 12. (Available in U.S. only) 24052-5 Pa. **$8.95**

COMPLETE BALLADES, IMPROMPTUS AND SONATAS, Frédéric Chopin. The four Ballades, four Impromptus and three Sonatas. Authoritative Paderewski edition. 240pp. 9 × 12. (Available in U.S. only) 24164-5 Pa. **$9.95**

NOCTURNES AND POLONAISES, Frédéric Chopin. 19 *Nocturnes* and 16 *Polonaises* reproduced from the authoritative Paderewski Edition for pianists, students, and musicologists. Commentary. viii + 272pp. 9 × 12. (Available in U.S. only) 24564-0 Pa. **$9.95**

COMPLETE MAZURKAS, Frédéric Chopin. 51 best-loved compositions, reproduced directly from the authoritative Kistner edition edited by Carl Mikuli. 160pp. 9 × 12. 25548-4 Pa. **$7.95**

FANTASY IN F MINOR, BARCAROLLE, BERCEUSE AND OTHER WORKS FOR SOLO PIANO, Frédéric Chopin. 15 works, including one of the greatest of the Romantic period, the Fantasy in F Minor, Op. 49, reprinted from the authoritative German edition prepared by Chopin's student, Carl Mikuli. 224pp. 8¾ × 11¼. 25950-1 Pa. **$7.95**

COMPLETE HUNGARIAN RHAPSODIES FOR SOLO PIANO, Franz Liszt. All 19 Rhapsodies reproduced directly from an authoritative Russian edition. All headings, footnotes translated to English. Best one volume edition available. 224pp. 8⅜ × 11¼. 24744-9 Pa. **$9.95**

ANNÉES DE PÈLERINAGE, COMPLETE, Franz Liszt. Authoritative Russian edition of piano masterpieces: *Première Année (Suisse): Deuxième Année (Italie)* and *Venezia e Napoli; Troisième Année,* other related pieces. 288pp. 9⅜ × 12¼. 25627-8 Pa. **$11.95**

COMPLETE ETUDES FOR SOLO PIANO, Series I: Including the Transcendental Etudes, Franz Liszt, edited by Busoni. Also includes Etude in 12 Exercises, 12 Grandes Etudes and Mazeppa. Breitkopf & Härtel edition. 272pp. 8⅜ × 11¼. 25815-7 Pa. **$11.95**

COMPLETE ETUDES FOR SOLO PIANO, Series II: Including the Paganini Etudes and Concert Etudes, Franz Liszt, edited by Busoni. Also includes Morceau de Salon, Ab Irato. Breitkopf & Härtel edition. 192pp. 8⅜ × 11¼. 25816-5 Pa. **$9.95**

SONATA IN B MINOR AND OTHER WORKS FOR PIANO, Franz Liszt. One of Liszt's most performed piano masterpieces, with the six Consolations, ten *Harmonies poetiques et religieuses,* two Ballades and two Legendes. Breitkopf and Härtel edition. 208pp. 8⅜ × 11¼. 26182-4 Pa. **$8.95**

PIANO TRANSCRIPTIONS FROM FRENCH AND ITALIAN OPERAS, Franz Liszt. Virtuoso transformations of themes by Mozart, Verdi, Bellini, other masters, into unforgettable music for piano. Published in association with American Liszt Society. 247pp. 9 × 12. 24273-0 Pa. **$9.95**

COMPLETE PIANO TRANSCRIPTIONS FROM WAGNER'S OPERAS, Franz Liszt. 15 brilliant compositions (1842–1882) on themes from *Rienzi, Flying Dutchman, Tannhäuser, Lohengrin,* other Wagnerian favorites. 176pp. 9 × 12. 24126-2 Pa. **$7.95**

COMPLETE WORKS FOR PIANOFORTE SOLO, Felix Mendelssohn. Breitkopf and Härtel edition of Capriccio in F# Minor, Sonata in E Major, Fantasy in F# Minor, Three Caprices, Songs without Words, and 20 other works. Total of 416pp. 9⅜ × 12¼. Two-vol. set. 23136-4, 23137-2 Pa. **$21.90**

COMPLETE SONATAS AND VARIATIONS FOR SOLO PIANO, Johannes Brahms. All sonatas, five variations on themes from Schumann, Paganini, Handel, etc. Vienna Gesellschaft der Musikfreunde edition. 178pp. 9 × 12. 22650-6 Pa. **$8.95**

COMPLETE SHORTER WORKS FOR SOLO PIANO, Johannes Brahms. All solo music not in other two volumes. Waltzes, Scherzo in E Flat Minor, Eight Pieces, Rhapsodies, Fantasies, Intermezzi, etc. Vienna Gesellschaft der Musikfreunde. 180pp. 9 × 12. 22651-4 Pa. **$7.95**

COMPLETE TRANSCRIPTIONS, CADENZAS AND EXERCISES FOR SOLO PIANO, Johannes Brahms. Vienna Gesellschaft der Musikfreunde edition, vol. 15. Studies after Chopin, Weber, Bach; gigues, sarabandes; 10 Hungarian dances, etc. 178pp. 9 × 12. 22652-2 Pa. **$8.50**

PIANO MUSIC OF ROBERT SCHUMANN, Series I, edited by Clara Schumann. Major compositions from the period 1830–39; *Papillons,* Toccata, Grosse Sonate No. 1, *Phantasiestücke, Arabeske, Blumenstück,* and nine other works. Reprinted from Breitkopf & Härtel edition. 274pp. 9⅜ × 12¼. 21459-1 Pa. **$12.95**

PIANO MUSIC OF ROBERT SCHUMANN, Series II, edited by Clara Schumann. Major compositions from period 1838–53; *Humoreske, Novelletten,* Sonate No. 2, 43 *Clavierstücke für die Jugend,* and six other works. Reprinted from Breitkopf & Härtel edition. 272pp. 9⅜ × 12¼. 21461-3 Pa. **$12.95**

PIANO MUSIC OF ROBERT SCHUMANN, Series III, edited by Clara Schumann. All solo music not in other two volumes, including *Symphonic Etudes, Phantaisie,* 13 other choice works. Definitive Breitkopf & Härtel edition. 224pp. 9⅜ × 12¼. 23906-3 Pa. **$10.95**

PIANO MUSIC 1888–1905, Claude Debussy. Deux Arabesques, Suite Bergamesque, Masques, first series of Images, etc. Nine others, in corrected editions. 175pp. 9⅜ × 12¼. 22771-5 Pa. **$7.95**

COMPLETE PRELUDES, Books 1 and 2, Claude Debussy. 24 evocative works that reveal the essence of Debussy's genius for musical imagery, among them many of the composer's most famous piano compositions. Glossary of French terms. 128pp. 8⅜ × 11¼. 25970-6 Pa. **$6.95**

PRELUDES, BOOK 1: The Autograph Score, Claude Debussy. Superb facsimile reproduced directly from priceless autograph score in Pierpont Morgan Library in New York. New Introduction by Roy Howat. 48pp. 8⅛ × 11. 25549-2 Pa. **$8.95**

PIANO MASTERPIECES OF MAURICE RAVEL, Maurice Ravel. Handsome affordable treasury; *Pavane pour une infante defunte, jeux d'eau, Sonatine, Miroirs,* more. 128pp. 9 × 12. 25137-3 Pa. **$6.95**

COMPLETE LYRIC PIECES FOR PIANO, Edvard Grieg. All 66 pieces from Grieg's ten sets of little mood pictures for piano, favorites of generations of pianists. 224pp. 9⅜ × 12¼. 26176-X Pa. **$10.95**

*Available from your music dealer or write for **free** Music Catalog to Dover Publications, Inc., Dept. MUBI, 31 East 2nd Street, Mineola, N.Y. 11501.*

1 7022